Living Out Titus 2

by

Woman to Woman Ministries

Living out Titus 2
By Woman to Woman Ministries

Table of Contents

Likewise, teach the older women to be reverent in the way they live, not to be slanderers or addicted to much wine, but to teach what is good. Then they can urge the younger women to love their husbands and children, to be self-controlled and pure, to be busy at home, to be kind, and to be subject to their husbands, so that no one will malign the word of God.

Titus 2:3-5

Introduction

Woman to Woman Ministries began in 2011 with the purpose of teaching and encouraging women using the Titus 2 principle. Through many emails, Facebook comments and blog comments, we continually hear two complaints of women. One, women don't have mentors and don't know how to go about getting them. And two, women don't know how to *be* mentors.

God didn't mean for us to do this life alone. Splattered all over His Word are bits of encouragement teaching us to connect with other believers.

Two are better than one, because they have a good return for their labor: If either of them falls down, one can help the other up. Ecclesiastes 4:9-10

As iron sharpens iron, so one man sharpens another. Proverbs 27:17

We need to have women in our lives that we look up to and turn to. Then on the flip side, we need to invest in the lives of other women. We pray that this book gives you the encouragement you need to live out Titus 2.

What is Titus 2:
Why Do I Need a Mentor?
By Shari Miller

Amanda, a young mother of 4, breathed a sigh of relief as she finally reached the checkout line at her local Wal-Mart, with her band of children in tow. Charlie, age 9, towered above the rest. His clothes were torn and dirty, and his face looked worn and tired. Jimmy, age 7, was coughing and his eyes watered, his voice could be heard echoing above the crowd as he kept asking, "When are we going to go home!" Max, age 3, looked scared as he clung to Amanda's leg. Those who passed by pointed and stared at the poor young boy. Baby Grace, just 6 months old, was fast asleep in the shopping cart, oblivious to what was going on around her.

Amanda was growing weary as she started placing new coats and clothes for the boys and groceries for dinner on the check stand. She could hear the people in line talking about her, "Look there is another mom on welfare, who does she think she is? I bet they all came from different dads too." Their harsh words and icy glares burrowed through her spirit. Tears started to fill her eyes as she tried to figure out how to get the card the state had given her to run through the machine at the stand. "Oh, please help me, Lord." she whispered.

Just then, the woman in line next to her, who Amanda recognized from her church, came up to lend her a hand, "I can help you with this. These new cards can be tricky." She smiled at Amanda, and looked at her children, in a calm and reassuring voice she said, "Are you a foster mom? I have 4 foster babies of my own." A sigh of relief fell from Amanda's lips as she said, "Yes, the three boys. They just came to our family over the weekend. They had no winter clothes, and I wanted to get something warm for them to wear." "You can do this." replied the woman, "It gets easier as time goes on. You are doing a great job! Keep up the good work!"

On the way home Amanda felt a wave of thankfulness rush over her. She knew in her heart that she and her husband were following the Lord's leading by taking the foster children into their home. She knew it would not be easy, but she was grateful for the older woman that God had put in her path to encourage her and help her at the store.

Amanda came from a broken home; this was all new territory for her. She was tired of trying to figure things out on her own. She wanted guidance to know how to be the best wife, mom, and friend she could be. The desired burned deep within her to learn as much as possible about how she could best serve her family and her Savior. She also knew that if she was going succeed, she needed to find other women who would guide her and show her the way.

Titus 2:4-5 states, *"Then they can urge the younger women to love their husbands and children, to be self-controlled and pure, to be busy at home, to be kind, and to be subject to their husbands, so that no one will malign the word of God."*

Ladies, God did not call us to be superwomen; He does not expect us to have everything figured out right from the beginning. He does, however, call us to learn from the older women in the church, to be mentored by them and to be shown the way that Christ wants us to live.

The dictionary defines a mentor as, "Someone who teaches or gives help and advice to a less experienced and often younger person." Having a mentor makes life so much easier. It's so comforting to know we can turn to someone who has already walked the road we are about to embark on. The Bible tells us five reasons why women need to have mentors.

1. To show us how love our husbands.

The fairy tales we grow up hearing about our prince charming coming to rescue us on a white horse are rarely true. True marriages are not portrayed on Hollywood movie screens. Marriage is hard work. It is an institution created by God to be lived with each person looking out for the other, and not themselves.

Marriage is not always a smooth path to walk on. It's beneficial to have someone in our corner who has had years of experience being married. They can teach us from past experiences and life lessons learned.

We can glean from their wisdom about how we can truly love our husbands regardless of the outside circumstances we face. When we don't have someone to show us the way, it is easy to get lost on the island of self where misery and gloom are constant companions.

2. To show us how love our children.

At first glance, motherhood seems so much easier than what is actually is. I can remember twenty some years ago telling my mom, "Mom, all I want is to be married and have a nice house, with a couple of children. Is that too much to ask?" No, it wasn't too much to ask, however, it was a lot harder than what I thought it would be.

When a new mom holds her baby in her arms for the first time, the feelings of love are enormous, surrounded by feelings of being completely overwhelmed. "How am I going to take care of my child? How do I get her to stop crying? Why isn't she nursing? When's the right time to start solid foods? Why isn't she crawling yet?"

These feelings can be enough to make a new mom stop dead in her tracks. But, the good news is, there is help! Seek out the older women in your church, family, and circle of friends that have been through this before. Ask their guidance on what they did when they were in your shoes. Glean from their knowledge and experience, rest in their words of comfort and encouragement. Times like these are when a mentor will boost your spirits and give you the strength to keep moving forward.

With time, maturity, and life giving words from friends, you will learn how to love and take care of your children according to God's plan.

3. To show us how be self-controlled and pure.

In the past my husband has called me, "His little bull dog." Why such a strange name you may ask? It's because I am very passionate about what I believe in and I was, at times, quick to let everyone one know that my way was the right way. I would stand for justice, and sometimes I would not do it in the most Christian way.

It took me time and the wisdom from my mentors to learn not to react without thinking. Through learning by example from the older women around me, I learned to slow down, think things through first, and to take it to the Lord in prayer. Without the example of my mentors, I would not be where I am today. It's not to say that I am perfect, I am far from that. However, I have grown tremendously by learning from the example of other Christian women that God has placed in my life.

4. To show us how to be kind.

Self-centeredness is a dangerous path on which to walk. When we get caught up in a "me first mentality," everyone suffers. God tells us in His word to not think of ourselves first, but rather to love others and the Lord.

"Love the Lord your God with all your heart and with all your soul and with all your mind and with all your strength.' The second is this: 'Love your neighbor as yourself.' There is no commandment greater than these." Mark 12:30-31

The way in which we practice this love to others, is by showing kindness through the power of Christ that dwells in us. As we look towards the older women in our church we can gain insight from what has worked for them, and how they have practiced kindness towards others in their lives. Whether it is practicing hospitality in our homes, caring for the sick, or visiting a shut in, we learn from the actions of others. We need to make sure we surround ourselves with Godly women, whose actions we can glean from.

5. To encourage us be busy at home.

"She selects wool and flax and works with eager hands. She is like the merchant ships, bringing her food from afar. She gets up while it is still night; she provides food for her family and portions for her female servants. She considers a field and buys it; out of her earnings she plants a vineyard. She sets about her work vigorously; her arms are strong for her tasks. She sees that her trading is profitable, and her lamp does not go out at night. In her hand she holds the distaff and grasps the spindle with her fingers. She opens her arms to the poor and extends her hands to the needy. When it snows, she has no fear for her household; for all of them are clothed in scarlet. She makes coverings for her bed; she is clothed in fine linen and purple. Her husband is respected at the city gate where he takes his seat among the elders of the land. She makes linen garments and sells them, and supplies the merchants with sashes. She is clothed with strength and dignity; she can laugh at the days to come. She speaks with wisdom, and faithful instruction is on her tongue. She watches over the affairs of her household and does not eat the bread of idleness. Her children arise and call her blessed; her husband also, and he praises her." -- Proverbs 31:13-28

Our duties as wives and mothers are specifically outlined in God's Word in the book of Proverbs. To be the woman God wants us to be, we need to have hands that are always busy with the tasks at home. The way we learn to do these tasks is through the teachings of mentors.

Just like a child needs to be taught how to read and write, we, too, need to learn from mentors who have gone before us. The tasks of cooking, and cleaning and child rearing may not come as second nature to some, especially if they were not taught it in their own home.

Do not let pride get in the way of asking for help. Seek out the advice of older women; let them know you what area you need help in.

6. To encourage us to be subject to our husbands.

When a young couple falls in love and gets married, the honeymoon phase is such a wonderful feeling. Neither can do wrong in the other ones eyes, that spark of romance is alive and well, and all you want to do is be with the love of your life in all your spare moments.

Then, out of nowhere it hits…that little thing that used to be endearing about your spouse now drives you crazy. You do not understand why he does the things he does and you are bound and determined to show him the right way, your way.

Wives, this is not how God called us to act. God calls us to be submissive to our husbands, "Wives, submit yourselves to your own husbands as you do to the Lord. For the husband is the head of the wife as Christ is the head of the church, his body, of which he is the Savior." Ephesians 5:22-23

Friends, our husbands deserve to be treated with honor and respect. We need to honor the decisions he makes for his family. We need to go to the Lord in prayer to seek out how the Father wants us to treat our man. We also need to look to the examples of older women who have been submissive to their husbands over the years.

God has specifically stated in His word how He wants Christian women to act. These words can be hard to put into practice if we have not had anyone acting them out before us.

Ladies, it's time to put the Superwoman cape away and open up our minds and hearts to the examples of others. We all need mentors in our lives to show us how to live according to Christ's word. If you do not have a mentor in your life, seek one out through prayer. The Lord will lead and guide you to the person that needs to speak words of wisdom, affirmation, and kindness to your weary soul. Just wait on Him, His timing His perfect; He knows what you need before you even ask for it.

The relationship between a young Christian woman and her mentor can establish strong foundations in the building of God's kingdom. It sets in place legacies to follow for those who come behind us, who are searching and yearning how to live the life God intended for them.

What is Titus 2:
Why Do I Need to Be a Mentor?
By Lisa Shaw

Thank you for caring about me, Lisa. Those words still resonate in my heart. The day Ann asked me to be her spiritual mentor I prayed first to be sure that this was something God wanted me to do. I knew He would want me to help her but I wanted His wisdom in this important task. I take the spiritual care of a person very seriously. We began working together and the first few months her struggles were being worked through; the pains of her past were being unfolded as she trusted God and began to grow in His Word. I took her under my wing and poured my love for God, His Word, my family and my life experiences (that applied to her needs), into Ann. Ann needed to understand how much Jesus loved her. She was a long time Christian with a wounded heart from the pains in her life and it had adversely affected her as a woman, a wife and a mother.

Over the course of a year, I had the privilege to mentor her spiritually and to help her to see how our spiritual lives directly impact our everyday living. Ann needed mentoring in how to apply biblical principles to everyday life. She also needed help in seeing herself through the lens of the Word and not the world. She learned how to engage God's love, and to love, trust and worship Him in return as she saw the words on the pages of the Bible become life to her. The more the Holy Spirit helped me to teach Ann from the Word and assist her with practical application; the more her life began to change. She learned how to study the Word and how to pray. She began to come out of a religious experience and grow in a relationship with Jesus Christ. This made her a better wife, mother and woman. It helped her to see that she was born with purpose and that God had plans for her that far exceeded her own thoughts. I remember the day she took my hand and said, *thank you for caring about me Lisa*, to which I replied, *it is my honor. God cares and so do I.* That is what mentoring is all about, caring about another person's well-being, and caring to the point of becoming actively involved in their lives as God leads you both.

My focus in this chapter is to help you to see yourself as a mentor regardless of your age, background, education or experience. God has put within you everything that you need to be a good mentor. It doesn't require you to have formal education or training, to be a pastor, or a bible scholar but it does require you to care.

The primary areas we will cover are:

1. The benefits of being a mentor

2. Mentoring spiritually with practical application

3. When you don't feel equipped to mentor

4. The life of a mentor

1. The benefits of being a mentor:

The primary benefit in being a mentor is that you have the privilege to honor God by pouring into the life of another woman. You get to be used by God to help her to be the best in the area in which she needs to be mentored.

Mentoring does not solely benefit the mentee but the mentor, as well, because as you pray, listen, teach, advise, counsel, support and encourage another person, it challenges you to continue to grow in your own relationship with God and your family. It also challenges you to grow in how you treat people at work, church, school and in the community. As you teach, you continue to learn. That's an important benefit to you as a mentor.

Mentoring does not mean you are responsible to change a life. Each person is accountable for their own behavior, however, mentoring does open the door for you to help someone who wants to be helped, and the benefits are far greater than you can imagine. A good example of the benefit of mentoring is found in the life of Timothy's grandmother, Lois, and his mother, Eunice.

"I thank God, whom I serve, as my ancestors did, with a clear conscience, as night and day I constantly remember you in my prayers. Recalling your tears, I long to see you, so that I may be filled with joy. I am reminded of your sincere faith, which first lived in your grandmother Lois and in your mother Eunice and, I am persuaded, now lives in you also. For this reason I remind you to fan into flame the gift of God, which is in you through the laying on of my hands. For the Spirit God gave us does not make us timid, but gives us power, love and self-discipline." 2 Timothy 1:3-6

We see generational influence in the passage above. I call it generational mentoring at its finest. A parent pours into a child who grows up, and pours into their own child and that child is then trained by a leader to do great things for the Kingdom of God. You have the benefit of pouring into your own children as well as into the lives of other women who are raising children. The impact creates a man or woman living for God. We see with Timothy and his spiritual leader, Paul. Paul teaches Timothy how to use the gifts God put in him for Kingdom purposes.

Who needs the gifts that God put into you? As a

Christian, mentoring is done with a biblically based foundation combined with practical application, and when the two are intertwined, the mentee grows in their walk with God and then God is honored.

2. Mentoring spiritually with practical application:

Let's look together at *Titus 2:3-5*. *"Likewise, teach the older women to be reverent in the way they live, not to be slanderers or addicted to much wine, but to teach what is good. Then they can urge the younger women to love their husbands and children, to be self-controlled and pure, to be busy at home, to be kind, and to be subject to their husbands, so that no one will malign the word of God."*

a.   Be reverent in the way that we live. That means having a personal, edifying and growing relationship with the Father, Son and Holy Spirit. It also means honoring God with our thought-life, our words, behavior, and treatment of our families and others. And when we fail, we must be quick to repent and get back in step with His Holy Spirit. *"Examine me, GOD, from head to foot, order your battery of tests. Make sure I'm fit inside and out. So I never lose sight of your love, but keep in step with you, I never missing a beat."* Psalm 26:2-3 (MSG)

b.   Discuss the Word of God and how to apply it in practical ways so that women will learn what is good and pleasing in the eyes of God in the care of their husbands, children and their household.

c.   A key component to mentoring is doing it with intentional love, compassion and a desire to influence and impact another woman's life so that she can be her best in the roles God allows her to live.

d.   It's also important, when mentoring, to remember to also help the mentee to learn to take better care of herself as a woman. One of the lessons I was not taught when I became a mother at 21 years old and then again at 28 years old was that taking care of me spiritually, physically and emotionally was just as important. I was brought up to believe that women should always put themselves on the back burner. God was first, then husband, children, serving in church, job responsibilities, and the needs of others; and then, if there is any ounce of energy left, take care of Lisa. Oh, but wait, do that load of laundry, clean that kitchen, even if it's late. Get everything ready for the next day and be superwoman. Don't get tired or sick, no time for it. Need a little rest? No time for it. It wasn't until Jesus spoke to my heart in a passage of Scripture that I realized I was out of balance. *"Love the Lord your God with all your heart and with all your soul and with all your mind and with all your strength. The second is this: 'Love your neighbor as yourself. There is no commandment greater than these.'" Mark 12:30-31*

Did you catch that? Jesus said to love God with every fiber of our being and then to love our neighbor as ourselves. He didn't say to love God and then everyone else instead of you. God is the priority and then loving others as ourselves. That means when I take better care of myself that makes me a better person, wife, mother and now, a grandmother, servant-leader and better at everything God has put in my hands. A good mentor will help a woman learn how to love God with all of her heart and then love others as she loves herself. In other words, teach her how to take care of her health and how to listen to the need for her body and mind to rest. Teach her not only the care of herself spiritually but, in all ways so that she can be her best in caring for those whom God puts in her path.

Now that we've looked at Titus 2, let's go through a few additional areas that are important to being a good mentor.

<u>Be available to God and to the mentee:</u>

God is looking for a heart that is available to Him and to the mentee. Be sure to communicate with the mentee and find out her needs. In other words, why does she desire for you to be her mentor. She may want to be mentored in developing a prayer life or learning how to study the Bible. She may need to be mentored in parenting, in being a wife, or in learning how to live a single life as a Christian woman. Mentoring can cover many areas. Be open to how God wants to use you.

<u>Think outside of the box:</u>

Find locations that work for both of you. Get creative with ways to mentor in addition to meeting, praying and studying the Word together. If you're mentoring a first time Mom, perhaps set a Saturday to have her over with the children. Show her some cooking tips for how to make meals in 30 minutes or less. I wish I had received that advice when I was a young Mom raising children. While you're cooking together, you can use that time to mentor her in some other aspects of being a wife, parenting or tending to her home. Or perhaps if you are mentoring a woman who is newly saved, go somewhere public for coffee, tea or water and as the Holy Spirit leads you, find someone to share your love with God in a personal and practical way as your mentee watches and perhaps engages. It will show her how easy it can be to just share God out of your own personal experiences.

Remember that being a mentor doesn't mean everything has to be very intense in spiritual teaching all the time. You are not her pastor. You are her mentor. You can, and should, mentor out of how God's Word works in your own life. Sharing personal experiences with your mentee builds your relationship. It fosters trust and transparency. This further enhances the mentoring.

<u>Listen attentively:</u>

Someone once said that listening is an art form. I'm not sure about that but I do believe that listening attentively is important and necessary in all of our relationships and that includes mentoring. I live by the quote, "People don't care how much you know until they know how much you care." I care. One of the ways I display that I care is to listen attentively. When we listen attentively it slows us down from giving quick answers. If listening attentively doesn't come naturally for you, pray and ask God to help you to cultivate this area of your life. Then, begin to practice giving your full attention in a conversation with your loved ones. I had to learn this early on in ministry because, by nature, I would begin to process as a person was speaking to me, and my mind would jump ahead, ready to help. That won't help a mentoring relationship.

Mentors are not supposed to know everything:

Mentoring does not mean we have all the answers. Only God does. If your mentee asks a question about a subject matter that you can't answer, be willing to say, *I don't know* but also be willing to say, *I'll find out*. That not only gains the trust of the mentee but it helps her to know that you are journeying together as Christian women.

Be honest about your own spiritual life:

Mentoring is not just what you teach or say but it includes leading by example. Being a mentor doesn't mean you will live a perfect life, however, we do want to lead by example. If you are encouraging a woman to live biblical principles, she must be able to see you live them as well. Credibility in mentoring is important. Be honest about your areas of flaw and imperfection as the Holy Spirit leads. Remember mentoring is not about the mentor, it's about the mentee. You don't want to burden your mentee with concerns from your private life. However, sharing some of the ways God has helped you helps the mentee to relate to another Christian woman.

Prayer:

As a Titus 2 mentor, praying for your mentor/mentee relationship is very important. Praying for your mentee's life in Christ is also important, and praying together is essential. It will help her to grow in her prayer life. It will give her a sense of comfort and strength that you are praying with her and it keeps God as the foundation of your mentoring relationship.

3. When you don't feel equipped to mentor:

You may be asking *Lisa, what if I don't feel equipped to mentor*. One of the many wisdom-tools I've learned in over three decades as a Christian is that most of what God uses me to do I don't feel equipped to do. What I've learned is that He is not looking for the qualified. He is looking for the willing and available person who

carries His heart of love. Once we say, "Yes, Lord," He then does the equipping.

Every experience you have endured; each mistake and triumph, tear and laughter that you can trace back in your mind, was not just for you to write in a journal or to share with someone you love. It is also so that you can reach your hand out to another person and say, *I care about you. Let me help you to be all that God has called you to be.*

Someone needs your love for God, your heart of compassion and the experiences you have acquired as a woman. We often think of mentoring as something done for young mothers, teens or young adults, however, mentoring is important at any age. Whether you are single, married, divorced or widowed, a mother, grandmother, auntie, sister or friend, God has put his love and compassion within you to extend not just to your family members, but to another woman who needs to be mentored.

If you wait until you feel equipped, you'll never become a mentor. If you wait until you have it all together in your life as a Christian, you'll never become a mentor. God is ready to use the willing heart. Are you willing? Someone needs what you have to offer them to help them to be their best.

4. The life of the mentor:

While being a mentor is not about being a perfect Christian, it is about living a life of humility before the Lord. Living with a bowed head, heart and home unto God makes us a good mentor. It's not just important how we live in our public lives but even more, what type of person we are in private. Character is still very important to God. The life of a mentor should reflect a heart pure in God.

Every good teacher is first a good student. To be an effective and efficient mentor, it is important that we remain good students of the Word of God for our own lives, and also have the appropriate biblical influences in our own lives.

There is power in God's Word. As a mentor you have the opportunity to help another woman to live His Word in the areas of her life where she desires help. His Word lights our way, imparts understanding and helps us to live the life He has purposed. *"The unfolding of your words gives light; it imparts understanding to the simple. Pray and ask God how He wants to use your life. Ask Him to put someone in your path that you can mentor. Don't be afraid. Remember mentoring is not about perfection or feeling qualified. Overcome any fear or concerns with God's help and step up and step out into the amazing path of helping another woman to become her best." Psalm 119:130 (ESV)*

I want to leave you with this, mentoring is life changing because as you mentor someone, it will positively affect the people in her life and, in turn, she will then mentor someone and so on. That is biblical change one life at a time, and that blesses people and honors God.

I'm excited about how God is going to use your heart, willingness and availability as a mentor. I am praying for you even now.

Living Titus 2 in Marriage
By Debi Baker

Titus 2 (GW)
"Tell believers to live the kind of life that goes along with accurate teachings. Tell older men to be sober. Tell them to be men of good character, to use good judgment, and to be well-grounded in faith, love, and endurance.

Tell older women to live their lives in a way that shows they are dedicated to God. Tell them not to be gossips or addicted to alcohol, but to be examples of virtue. In this way they will teach young women to show love to their husbands and children, to use good judgment, and to be morally pure. Also, tell them to teach young women to be homemakers, to be kind, and to place themselves under their husbands' authority. Then no one can speak evil of God's word.

Encourage young men to use good judgment. Always set an example by doing good things. When you teach, be an example of moral purity and dignity. Speak an accurate message that cannot be condemned. Then those who oppose us will be ashamed because they cannot say anything bad about us.

Tell slaves who are believers to place themselves under their masters' authority in everything they do. Tell them to please their masters, not to argue with them or steal from them. Instead, tell slaves to show their masters how good and completely loyal they can be. Then they will show the beauty of the teachings about God our Savior in everything they do.

After all, God's saving kindness has appeared for the benefit of all people. It trains us to avoid ungodly lives filled with worldly desires so that we can live self-controlled, moral, and godly lives in this present world. At the same time we can expect what we hope for—the appearance of the glory of our great God and Savior, Jesus Christ. He gave himself for us to set us free from every sin and to cleanse us so that we can be his special people who are enthusiastic about doing good things.

Tell these things to the believers. Encourage and correct them, using your full authority. Don't let anyone ignore you."

This eBook was written to give encouragement to women of all ages. In this chapter we will deal with living according to Titus 2 standards in our marriage. We will be focusing specifically on verses 3-5.

So, how do we live like we are instructed in Titus 2 in our marriage? First of all, we must look at the passage and dissect it a bit. Paul is writing this letter to Titus in order to describe the requirements and duties of elders and bishops.

In verse 4, Paul says the older woman is told to train the younger woman to love her husband, and in verse 5, Paul goes on to say that she is to train the younger woman to be submissive to her husband. It says that the older woman is to "train" the younger woman to love her husband. Have you ever thought about what this is really saying?

Let's look at what the word 'train' means. It means to make proficient by instruction and practice. So, the older woman is to train... to make capable by instruction and practice...the younger woman. It stands to reason that we don't need someone to train us in something that we have already mastered. We can also make the assumption from this passage that loving according to God's standards is something that does not come naturally. We know that we are born with the innate desire to please one's self. It is not 'natural' to put others before self. The ability to do that happens only when we come to know Christ and His putting US before Himself. When Christ is the head of our life, the Holy Spirit will help us to be able to put others before self...including our husbands.

If we are honest with ourselves, I think we would all admit that we want the fairytale ending in our marriage...*happily ever after!* Unfortunately, that doesn't just happen. It takes work. Anyone who says marriage is a 50/50 situation has never been married. Well, at least not successfully married. You see, marriage is 100/100! Period!

We want our husbands to put us on a pedestal and treat us like a queen. Well, I did. I didn't know I did, but I did. It was many years ago. We hadn't been married a long time but still several years. I was attending a ladies devotional group at church. It was led by my pastor's wife whom I loved and respected so much. We were studying a book that I cannot remember the name of right now but on this particular day we were discussing this very topic...loving our husband BEFORE self. Well, I was having trouble with this. It wasn't so much that I wanted to be on that proverbial pedestal but I didn't think I should 'have' to bow to him! My beloved pastor's wife was so patient with me and I am ever appreciative to her for her gentle training! No, I don't *have* to bow down to him and give in to his every whim. The difference comes when I 'choose' to love him and put him first!

This particular incident is a prime example of living Titus 2 in my marriage. My pastor's wife was willing to teach and I was teachable. Once I learned that it was my choice and that everything won't always be rosy in my marriage, I began to be able to grow...as a woman and as a wife.

Ok, so one of the biggest things I learned was that while I can have that happily ever after fairytale ending, every day may not be perfect. We have to remember that the fairytale ending is pretty unrealistic. While we were dating the man that would one day become our husband, we were smitten with him. We probably thought he was perfect. Now, you are married and suddenly he isn't so perfect. Perhaps he thought we were perfect, too. I'm sure he is finding out that we are not! The best thing we can do is remember that he is not perfect. Life in the courting/dating phase is not 'real' life. Life isn't perfect...love isn't perfect.

I'm sure that there are lots of things we'd like to change in our spouses. Instead of sulking about the fact that he isn't perfect after all, remember YOU aren't perfect either. You also need to be praying that God will help you to become the wife you are supposed to be. Notice I didn't say to pray that God would make your husband into the husband he is supposed to be! It isn't up to you to decide if he is or isn't being what God wants him to be. That, my friend, is between him and God.

Praying for God to change our spouse so that we don't have to change is selfish! Instead of praying that way, we need to pray for their relationship with God. Once his relationship with God is on the right track, God will begin to produce in him the changes that need to take place. It is important that we remember to ask God to change US and only us. Praying that He will change us will cause us to become more accepting of our spouse. And I can almost promise you that as God works in YOU, the things that had bothered you about your husband will seem less important than before.

Another very important thing to remember is that marriage is supposed to be for life. God never intended marriage to be throw away. In today's world, 1 in 2 marriages end in divorce...including those marriages in the church! That statistic is horrendous! Listen, marriage is WORK! You can't work at a relationship during the dating/courting phase and then once the 'I do's' are said stop working on it! What if we treated our job like we do our marriage? Would we have that job for very long? What if we spent the amount of time with our kids that we do working on our relationship with our spouse? Would they be properly raised? If we don't put the time in to working on our marriage, it won't last! Remember, I said earlier, marriage is 100/100 ALL THE TIME! You have to give 100% of yourself ALL THE TIME to your marriage and he has to give 100% of himself ALL THE TIME!

Another thing to remember, particularly if you have kids, is that you need to continue to date AFTER you are married. I can't stress this enough! I am going to share something very personal with you. It is directly related to this topic. Some many years ago, my in-laws celebrated their 25th wedding anniversary. Now, my in-laws were the kind of people that always welcomed anyone into their home. At any given time there was someone other than their own children living in their home. Well, they celebrated their 25th anniversary and 2 weeks later, they were separated. Why? Because in their 25 years of marriage, they never dated. He did his thing and she did hers. For the first time in their entire marriage they had no one living in their home. All the kids were grown and there were no 'extras' living with them. They had become strangers in their own home. Thankfully, they reconciled and remained together until the death of my father-in-law. The point is this...DATE YOUR MATE!!!

On the other side of that coin is another personal story. My husband and I have 4 children. They are all grown now and we have 10 beautiful grandchildren! While our kids were young, my husband and I dated every week! Of the 2 weekend nights (Friday/Saturday), one was spent with our kids and one with each, other on a date. Now, the date nights may not always have been just me and him but they were always without the kids. We may not have always done something 'special' but we always did something together. It could have been as simple as taking a drive in the country or walking in the local mall; it was something that allowed us to participate in each other. Now that our kids are grown and out of the house, we still have a thriving relationship. We are more in love today than we were on our wedding day some 37 ½ years ago! Dating your mate is vital to a successful marriage. You don't have to spend money...just time! If going 'out' is completely out of the question, put the kids to bed and spend some quality time together at home...talk, touch...the activity isn't important...being together is. Remember, you will get out of your marriage exactly what you put in to it!

It is also important to remember that we must not demean our man. We are to lift him up, NOT put him down. Some dear friends of ours called it 'kidding on the square.' When you 'joke around' at the expense of your spouse, it is degrading. A man needs to know that his wife thinks he is special. If we are determined to be a Titus 2 woman in our marriage, esteem your mate!!! Think how you would feel if your husband put you down or embarrassed you in front of your friends or his? Don't...please...don't stoop to this level. Go back to praying for him...not that he would change but that his relationship with God would be first and foremost in his life. When God is first, He will be able to work in your husband's life.

Finally, keep in mind that love is a choice and not a feeling. When you began your relationship with your spouse, it was most likely because there was a mutual attraction between you. That attraction grew from that 'feeling' into a choice to continue the relationship. There will be times when you don't 'feel' like loving the man sitting across the dinner table. How you choose to react in those times will determine your character. If you think about it, we all have those family members that we love because they are family but sometimes we don't like them very much. Love is something we choose to do; like...now that's another story. {smiles} When those times arise and you don't *'feel'* like loving him, pray and ask God to show you how to love him even more!

I fully believe that many of today's marital problems are directly related to the failure of the couple to live according to the commands written in Scripture, particularly those commands to love and respect one another. I honestly believe that if we could begin to see beyond the world's idea of 'me, me, me,' then we could understand that our husband is a gift from God. If we can put our own selfish pride behind us and live like Titus 2 directs, our marriages would be so much better.

I pray, sweet sister, that you will take the words of Paul to heart. Don't wallow in what your husband isn't doing but rather begin to do what you know in your heart that God wants *you* to do. Treat him like a king and he will treat you like his queen.

Living Titus 2 in Parenting
By Jenilee Goodwin

"Miss Jan?" my 8 year old asked. "What is this drawer for?"

"Well, that is called my junk drawer." Miss Jan answered.

"What is a junk drawer?" Annalise curiously continued her questions.

"It is a drawer that you put all kinds of things in that you want to keep close but don't necessarily use every day. Things like pens and pencils and rubber bands... that kind of stuff."

Annalise quietly continued her perusal of the newly discovered junk drawer. A few minutes later I heard her sweet voice float through the kitchen. "Wow... Miss Jan!" she happily exclaimed. "How many matches do you have in here?"

I smiled to myself from the bathroom where I was curling my hair. We were in the midst of our missions support raising travels and were once again staying with friends from a local church. Our whole family had never stayed in this particular home before so everything was new for the girls.

I smiled because as Annalise popped out funny question

after funny question to Jan about her junk drawer, Jan patiently answered each and every one. Jan allowed Annalise to stand in her kitchen and pull her junk drawer apart, letting Annalise hold things up for everyone to see.

Now, a junk drawer is personal space. Really...anyone can stick anything in a junk drawer. It is the drawer you throw things in from the counter that you don't want visiting friends to see. It is a drawer full of silly randomness; full of those things loosely termed valuable but more than likely things that should have been thrown away, hence the term "junk" in its name.

Mixed in with the important things like extra pens, a needed receipt and a few rubber bands can be an old key or a sticky penny or a scribbled on note pad from 1993. You never know what you might find in someone's junk drawer. It takes courage to permit someone to dig through your kitchen junk drawer. It takes a confidence and an allowance to be real.

As I've thought more about that junk drawer moment, I began thinking about Titus 2. I thought about the challenge for older women to teach younger women. Titus 2:3-5 *reads, "Likewise, teach the older women to be reverent in the way they live... Then they can urge the younger women to love their husbands and children, to be self-controlled and pure, to be busy at home, to be kind, and to be subject to their husbands, so that no one will malign the word of God."*

I started thinking about how this applies to parenting. The model set for us in Titus 2 really is a perfect model for women to learn from other women in the art of parenting.

Parenting is an art. It is something learned and grown and developed. Parenting doesn't always come naturally, even though we think it should. Parenting doesn't come with a "How To" book or a step-by-step instruction manual even though that would be an amazing help to new moms and dads all over the world.

Parenting is close knit. Parenting is gut-level and a

minute-by-minute test of endurance. Parenting is hard and rough and always challenging. Parenting is a God-given self-help, self-discovery, and self-growth process. Parenting will chisel you and mold you and make you into God's ideal for your life. Parenting will help you clearly see your own faults, difficulties and struggles in the perfect, pure blessing of your children.

Because of the in-depth nature of parenting, we need the model of women who have walked this road before and survived.

We need to see their tips and tricks, their victories and failures, their tears and joys. We need to get an uninterrupted view of their parenting "junk drawer." By this real, transparent model, we will learn ways of parenting that are otherwise unseen and untaught.

We need to hear the stories of how their toddlers refused to learn the word "no." We need to know that at one time their children ran in church and embarrassed them in the grocery store. We need to hear how they agonized over the proper way to talk about sex with their daughters and how they struggled to find the right words when their sons asked deep questions about love. We need to know that they prayed for wisdom as they watched a child rebel or as they rocked a crying, sick baby at 2am. We need to know their junk, hear their messy places and cry with their joyous accounts of victory over trial in their children's lives.

Young women need to have uninterrupted access into the heart of a seasoned mom. They need permission to dig through the seasoned mom's junk drawer of parenting stories. They need to be able to ask silly questions and get honest answers.

Titus 2 allows for a vulnerable parenting model that thrives on trust, time and truth. Titus 2 gives older women permission to share their deepest dreams and fears while challenging younger women to listen with open ears and yearning hearts. Titus 2 gives guidance to the ever-increasing cultural independence of women and brings balance to the thought that parenting tips can go out of style. **Biblical models of parenting never go out of style**. Why? Because whether the parenting tip worked or flat out failed, older women and younger women alike can learn something of value as they line up each and every tip with God's Word.

The beauty of this thought reminds us that seasoned mothers who have prodigal sons and daughters still have an important place in the Titus 2 parenting model. Older moms who feel like everything they knew about parenting is out of date and tired... your input is valuable. Young mothers, you have an obligation to glean and to learn and to listen. As new moms, you are learning things everyday that will help and benefit other moms around you. The truth is we all have a voice, a place, and an ability to share and learn together.

When I think of Jan standing in her kitchen, talking to Annalise and showing her the inside her junk drawer, I think about how simple Titus 2 learning can be. Annalise was open to learn and Jan was open to teach. Even more than that, Annalise, in her genuine attitude, was able to add her thoughts into the conversation, too!

Titus 2 in Parenting

First, let's define older women, as the Bible mentions, in the parenting scenario. The "older" would mean a woman who has had children or is past the stage of another mom. If you've been there before, you are "older" in the experience of parenting.

Next, let's define younger women, again as the Bible says it, in the parenting scenario. The "younger" would mean a woman who is in a stage behind another woman, a woman who is at an earlier point in parenting.

When I was a new mom, I remember feeling like I was the only person on the planet to be exhausted from late night feedings, to wear clothes stained with spit up, or to feel alone from talking to toddlers all day long. I often felt like I was the only one feeling completely disorganized and out-of-touch with reality. I felt like life was going to be hard forever and my diaper days would never end. It was hard to relate to older moms who seemed 'put together' like they'd never had a long day busy with mothering in their lives.

I remember very vividly one day in particular. I was sitting out in the hot sun wearing an old brown tank top with stretchy, light-weight shorts and some cheap flip flops. I felt frumpy and sticky and very mom-like. The girls were playing in the fountains of a local nice, beautiful shopping area. The fountains sit right next to a gorgeous restaurant. Walking into the restaurant were women dressed in trendy pantsuits and adorable skirts with heels. Heels were the last thing I'd dream of wearing at that stage in my life. Heels, 3 babies under the age of 3 and diaper bags do not mesh well. Not to mention how rarely I even have an opportunity to dress up! I sat there thinking, "Do these women even remember being a new, young mom? Did they have days like this? Will I one day feel put together and get to enjoy lunch at a beautiful restaurant?"

I hoped they did. I hoped they could see me with my children and smile. I hoped that if I had a chance to talk to them, they would take time to share with me their mommy memories, tips and thoughts. As a young mom, I wanted understanding, love and care from other women who could relate to who and where I was in my life.

I purposed in that moment to make sure that I would never forget what it is like to be a new mom with babies and toddlers. As my girls get older, I make an effort to not forget the potty training days, the tooth loosing days, the starting school days, and so on. I don't want to forget because, in remembering, I cannot only offer advice, but I can offer compassion, encouragement, help and prayer.

Remembering previous parenting seasons gives me the ability to truly relate with a mom in a season I've already walked through. I can remember the feeling of tiredness that comes with new mom days. I can remember the frustrations of teaching toddlers not to hit or bite. I can recall the utter loneliness that can sometimes accompany new motherhood days. I will remember the pain and beauty of nursing a newborn. I will remember the gritty reality of repetitive discipline and creative thinking that are a normal part of mothering children.

Sometimes the value of an older mom remembering and commiserating with you can be better than any other piece of offered advice.

Now, that isn't to say that advice isn't needed. Oh, it is. It is a very much needed and necessary and a real part of Titus 2.

Older moms need to be ready and available to share bits of wisdom, tricks of the trade, ways of doing things and proven methods of parenting with younger moms. Some of the most basic advice from an older mom is what truly got me through many of my young mom days. An older mom would say a phrase or give a tip that would work for me and I would be on cloud nine for days because I found something that helped me in my situation.

It is through these relationships with women who've gone before us or women who are coming behind us that this Titus 2 model plays out in real life.

We have an opportunity, ladies, to be the church to each other. We can be God's hands of love to a new mom by helping her learn how to nurse or cloth diaper a baby or get spit up stains out of laundry. We can be an example of kindness by offering to babysit or hold a crying baby in church. We can physically be the support another mom needs. We can be an ear to listen, a shoulder to cry on, a friend to pray with or a hand to help. Moms, we can be this to each other as we parent our children.

We each hold within us powerful, valuable information that should be shared. Sometimes, though, our busy and full lives don't always allow for this to happen. We can be so wrapped up in the season we are in that we can forget to seek out advice or we can forget to share advice. Sometimes our "junk drawer" of mistakes and struggles and pain can keep us from feeling like we have anything to learn or to offer. We can isolate ourselves and forget that God provided a ready-made support system through other women. We can be afraid to share our needs or our thoughts, wondering how other women will respond to our questions or our advice.

The Titus 2 parenting model encourages us to step away from those fears and be willing to live life in the vulnerability of openness. Living our lives in a way that makes sure we have time to pour into new moms or to stop and ask a question if we are struggling in motherhood. The Bible encourages us to let God use our junk and allow Him to make it a tool another woman can learn from.

To boil this all down, we, as moms in any season of parenting, can learn and can listen. We can be open and ask questions and offer help. We all have a part in the biblical model of Titus 2 parenting.

A final thought in Titus 2 parenting? Prayer. Women, let's pray for each other as mothers and as parents. We all know the difficult job we face to raise our children in the Lord. Some days, the battle just seems extremely difficult and more than we can handle. The overwhelming motherhood days of little ones or middle schoolers or teenagers seem so very long and sometimes never-ending.

There are times to teach and times to listen but there is always time to pray, to lift each other up in the way only another mother can do. When you aren't sure what advice to give? Pray. When you don't know the right words to say in comfort to another precious mother? Pray. When you feel like you are inadequate to help? Pray. When you feel like you are too young to have input or too old to understand? Pray.

Ephesians 3:16-21 has a beautiful model for prayer that I

think we can adapt to fit each other as women raising children. It certainly covers each situation we face in a wonderful way.

It says, *"I pray that out of his glorious riches he may strengthen you with power through his Spirit in your inner being, so that Christ may dwell in your hearts through faith. And I pray that you, being rooted and established in love, may have power, together with all the Lord's holy people, to grasp how wide and long and high and deep is the love of Christ, and to know this love that surpasses knowledge—that you may be filled to the measure of all the fullness of God. Now to him who is able to do immeasurably more than all we ask or imagine, according to his power that is at work within us, to him be glory in the church and in Christ Jesus throughout all generations, forever and ever! Amen."*

Moms, can we pray that for each other? Pray for strength. Pray that we will feel God's presence through our mothering days. Pray that we will sense God's love for us and our families. Pray that we might be full of God and that we would see God do miraculous things in our lives. Pray that God's glory would be brightly evident in our lives as our families strive to serve God together.

Living Titus 2 in Homemaking
By Jami Balmet

Homemaking is quickly becoming a lost art. The days when our Grandmother's would spend hours making sure their home was an inviting environment where the Gospel could flourish are long gone. Instead, homemakers are ridiculed in popular media and looked down upon as "only" stay at home moms or "housewives."

Most young women today are entering marriage without even the most basic homemaking skills such as cooking, cleaning, and meal planning let alone those special homemaking touches which truly make a house a home!

It has become such a burden on my heart that within the church we need to be intentionally preserving the art of homemaking as women. Developing intentional Titus 2 relationships with both older and younger women around us needs to be one of our top priorities as homemakers.

A Note to Younger Women

Young women, are you hurting for mentorship? Do you want to create a Gospel Centered home but are not sure where to start? Seek out older women.

As a young woman, I know it can sometimes feel like there are no godly older women to teach you the skills of homemaking, and while it can seem like that in our feminist culture, the older women are there. We just have to intentionally seek them.

Keep your eyes and your ears open for these older women. Intentionally seek to build relationships with older women, invite them over for coffee. Start observing and don't be afraid to initiate a relationship with older women, don't wait for them to make the first move!

A Note to Older Women

Older women, has God laid a burden on your heart to help younger women but you feel like the younger women are not interested, too busy, etc? Remember, as a young woman, it can be difficult sometimes to ask for help.

Try to keep an eye out for that young mother at church who is trying to keep it all together Sunday morning, the one who appears to have it all under control, and the one who is juggling two babes while seeming to pay attention to the sermon. Look for that one who is hurting on the inside for someone to tell her that it's okay for days to be tough right now. It's okay to feel lonely sometimes even when you are surrounded by kids all day. It's okay to ask for and receive help.

Older women, remember what it's like. Be bold and reach out to a new wife and offer to get together for a baking day. Offer babysitting so the young mom of three can get out of the house and grocery shop by herself. Remember what it's like...and live life alongside the young women.

What is a Homemaker?

This question comes up for me nearly every week. I have a passion for Biblical Homemaking and love to share my thoughts, ideas, and tips on creating a Gospel Centered Home. Many women approach me and share that they wish they could be "homemakers" but until they have kids, they have to work outside the home. There is also the single mother who desires to spend more time creating fancy meals and creating a warm environment in her home but she feels like a failure since she "can't be a homemaker."

My heart breaks for these women - not because they can't spend more time cooking and decorating - but because they miss the entire <u>definition of what a homemaker is</u>. A homemaker is not defined by the amount of hours you spend at home, the number of homemade meals you make each week or by the quality and quantity of your homemade crafts and home decor projects.

A homemaker is not simply an occupation; rather it's a God-given role to all women. You don't stop being a homemaker because at this point in your life you are not married. You don't stop being a homemaker when your husband dies and you are forced to return to work. And you don't stop being a homemaker when you have four children under the age of six and it's all you can do to pop a frozen pizza into the oven before your husband walks in the door and dishes fill the sink and laundry piles the floor.

Homemaking is a career for all women, regardless of whether they also happen to work outside the home during this stage of life or is married or have children. Homemaking is that special skill set which prepares a woman to love her family, nourish her family, care for her family, pray for her family, and create a Gospel Centered home.

"Homemaking is indeed a career in the sense that it demands a woman's careful diligence in preparation, dedicated commitment to priorities associated with the assignment, freshest energy, and keenest creativity. Most dictionaries define the homemaker as 'one who manages a household especially as a wife and mother.' Though the homemaker does her job with no expectation of a salary (much less financial bonuses and perks), she cannot duplicate her services for any amount of money." - The Christian Homemaker's

Handbook, page 21

<u>Being a homemaker</u> takes creativity, energy, and lots of hard work and determination. It's not an easy job. Many in our society today look down upon the homemaker, imagining her in a somewhat slothful occupation, whittling the days away reading books, taking naps, and making a batch of cinnamon rolls every once in a while.

But anyone who has <u>managed a home</u> before knows that it is a full time job that never ends. While being a homemaker is the most rewarding role that we can fill, it is also a thankless and exhausting job at times.

We Can't Do It Alone

A common mistake that women make today is that they try and live this life independently. We want to be superwoman. We want to be able to flawlessly handle each day's tasks with style and elegance. We imagine a perfect home, with well behaved children, home baked bread and a four course meal on the table each night. But the reality is, five minutes into our day and we want to cry. Our house is in disarray, our children our fighting and screaming, we forgot to go grocery shopping, we can't even see our sink it's so full of dishes, and we pop a frozen pizza into the oven for dinner...again.

Women no longer live in community with one another. It used to be that when a new mother brought her baby home from the hospital, she was surrounded for months and years with helpful mothers, grandmothers, and older women from church lending help and advice when needed. Women didn't need Google or Pinterest back then because they were surrounded by real life homemakers who were teaching them the skills and virtues of being a homemaker.

"*When a woman chooses to pursue homemaking with energy, imagination, and skill, she accepts a challenging task. As well as meeting the mundane needs of her family efficiently and completely, she also often finds the time to enrich lives with her tender loving care - encouraging and guiding, counseling, or comforting. She is available to divide sorrow or share rejoicing, making the ones most dear to her the first priority in time and the most important work of her life."* - The Christian Homemaker's Handbook, page 21

There is so much to learn and juggle as a homemaker, wife, and mother. Learning how to have a vibrant spiritual life with the Lord and live this out in your home cannot be learned simply through reading. Sermons, books, and other resources can give you the building blocks you need to understand the Scriptural basis behind our theology and why homemaking is such a high calling for woman - but you will never truly understand how to live out this role until you observe a godly older woman living it out, day by day.

"I don't think it takes a rocket scientist to know that men and women are different. God's truth is the same, but our gender sometimes determines how that truth is pushed out into life. No man understands experientially how it feels to be a wife, to have a menstrual cycle, to have a baby, or to go through menopause. Paul was smart enough to know that women need women to train them how to apply God's Word to areas of our lives that are uniquely feminine. In this command, older women are given the high calling of traditioning Biblical womanhood. This is not a ministry of minutia; it is a vital part of church life that must not be pushed to the back-burner." - Spiritual Mothering, page 45.

Living out Titus 2 in Homemaking

So what does this all mean on a daily, practical level? **Homemaking is an art and career that takes intentional time, commitment, and hard work to cultivate.** As women, we cannot live this life in solitude. Titus 2 commands us to live our lives with and learn from older women. Likewise, older women, you are commanded to open up and share your life and experiences with younger women around you. These commands are not optional, so what are you doing about it?

Make a List

When looking at homemaking as an art and a career, you

have to be intentional about it. If you want to be a godly homemaker, it isn't just going to happen. You have to work towards that goal. In order to grow into your goal as a Christian

Homemaker, you have to first know what that goal *is*.

My list for what an ideal homemaker is might look slightly different than yours. The foundation of what a godly homemaker is should be the same, taken straight out of Scripture but how certain parts of that play out, depend upon your personality, talents, and skills. Of course, the perfect model of a Christian homemaker is the Proverbs 31 woman:

*"An excellent wife who can find? She is far more precious than jewels...She **seeks** wool and flax, and **works** with willing hands...She **rises** while it is yet night and **provides** food for her household and portions for her maidens. She **considers** a field and buys it; with the fruit of her hands she **plants** a vineyard. She **dresses** herself with strength and makes her arms strong. She **perceives** that her merchandise is profitable. Her lamp does not go out at night. She **puts** her hands to the distaff, and her hands **hold** the spindle. She **opens** her hand to the poor and **reaches** out her hands to the needy."* - Proverbs 31:10-20

Does your life have to look exactly like this excellent wife? In order to be a godly homemaker, do you have to buy a field and plant a vineyard? Of course not. Look beyond those details, what do you see? I see a woman who works hard looking after the best interests of her family. She is kind and generous, providing food for her entire household. She serves the poor and needy by sacrificing her time and resources. She is constantly looking forward to make sure she is ready for what is coming, but she also takes care of today's tasks with determination and love. **This is a Titus 2 woman you could learn from.**

Young women start a list of the skills and virtues that you want to develop. Is your family surviving on frozen burritos and fast food? Develop specific goals that you want to achieve with Gospel intent. Would you like to minister to families in your church and neighborhood by <u>inviting them over for a meal</u>? On your list, make a goal of learning how to cook yummy and nutritious meals for large groups.

Seek Out Older Women

With this list in mind, start working towards your goals. Pinterest, Google, and books can be helpful, but there is nothing like learning from a real life homemaker who has been honing these skills for forty years. One of my personal goals is to learn how to sew so that I can save money and make modest clothing for my family. But sewing is becoming a lost art so I am always on the lookout for older women who know how to sew and don't mind spending a few hours teaching me.

I so often hear young women complaining that there are no older women to teach them. And older women feel outdated and unneeded by the younger generations. So whether you are younger or older and looking for mentoring relationships try and start with a friendship. Living out life alongside other women is often the best way to learn how to be better homemakers, whether or not you have a formal "mentoring" relationship.

Older and younger women, be bold and seek out other women to be in relationship with. If you feel like you don't know any godly women, try inviting someone who you only casually know over for coffee this week. Keep doing that, and over time you will start to develop friendships and lasting relationships with other women.

<u>Practice hospitality</u> and invite an older couple over for dinner with your whole family. Go out of your way during Sunday school to ask the new wife how she is settling into married life. During the church potluck, offer to hold the new mama's baby so she can eat in peace for a few minutes and ask her how she has been adjusting. Volunteer with your widow's ministry and offer to write letters or stop in and say hi to the widows in your church.

Developing mentoring relationships with other women means you will put yourself out there and probably feel vulnerable. You might feel awkward and gasp! the other woman might even find out that you are not perfect! But this is how authentic relationships form, grow, and blossom into mutually edifying mentorship.

Develop a Homemaking Group or Program

Developing a homemaking group can be a wonderful way to have fun, develop relationships with peers and older women, and learn essential homemaking skills. As I've been intentional about connecting with other women my age and stage in life (wives and mothers with young children) it has become apparent that women are hungry to learn how to be godly homemakers.

My group of friends has decided that we would learn these homemaking skills together! We get together each week at one of our houses and work on different homemaking projects. During the summer when tomatoes were ripe, we got together and our friend who is a master at canning taught us all how to make and can spaghetti sauce. We had a great time together and we all left with a few cans of delicious spaghetti sauce.

This works out well for us because we all have small children and kid proof houses. We set our kids up in the living room with lots of toys and between all the moms; someone has an eye on the kids at all times. During these times of baking, cooking, or working on other projects, we have time to talk and bond together. We learn from each other how to best put our babies down for a nap, the cheapest places to buy healthy groceries, and fun ways to play with our kids and make time for our husbands.

Developing a program or group like this is our first intentional step towards becoming Godly homemakers. We also have goals of bringing older women into our group to help teach a lesson such as sewing or quilting. If you are having a hard time finding older mentors, then maybe you can start a group like this of your friends and peers and make goals of brining older women into your group eventually.

Homemaking Matters

"In a sense the homemaker has been sidelined for more than half a century. She is considered a nonperson by many who do not see value in her work. She does not have what others consider a respectable title for her position, and she lacks a clear job description of what is considered worthwhile work. She does not receive a salary for her work. She just does what needs to be done to get the job done...Most believe that the biblical model for a homemaker, who devotes her freshest energies and most of her time to keeping her home, is obsolete." - The Christian Homemaker's Handbook, page 19

Don't believe the lies of our world that say the life of a homemaker doesn't matter. Don't buy into the judgment that you have to have a corporate career in order to be "worth" something. The calling of the wife and mother is a high and noble calling. Homemakers do have worth and what they do has eternal importance in the Kingdom of God.

"From cover to cover, the Bible exalts women. In fact, it often seems to go out of the way to pay homage to them, to ennoble their roles in society and family, to acknowledge the importance of their influence, and to exalt the virtues of women who were particularly godly examples." - John MacArthur, The Biblical Portrait of Women

So this week I challenge you to take a look at your life and the life of the Proverbs 31 woman. Of course, none of us can be perfect and we shouldn't be trying to achieve perfection, but what areas of homemaking do you need help in? Be honest and try to lay aside the "superwoman" ideal where you do everything yourself and exclude authentic relationships with other women in your life.

Make a list of what areas you need and want to improve upon in your quest towards becoming a godly homemaker and then invite a woman into your home for coffee and make a start towards intentional, Gospel-Centered mentoring.

Living Titus 2 in the Kitchen
By Leah Hostetler

I love Proverbs 31! It is so full of traits that I want to improve on and learn.

> *She gets up before dawn to prepare breakfast for her household and plan the day's work for her servant girls.*
> *Proverbs 31:15 NLT*

And who doesn't want their husband and children to rise and call them blessed and praise them?

Her children arise up, and call her blessed; her husband also, and he praiseth her. Proverbs 31:28 KJV

Proverbs 31 can seem a little daunting and unattainable if we try to become all that this woman is that is described in this chapter, but give yourself time, read a verse a week, and work on acquiring that trait this week, read another verse the following week and work on that. Don't stop reading a new verse every week just because you feel like you haven't achieved the previous one. It's a journey we are all on, keep going and eventually you will see yourself (with God's help of course) become more and more like the woman described here! Let it spill out and bless others lives as well. Find a friend to do it with you and share every week how it has blessed you and what you are learning.

Now, back to the actual topic I am writing about: **THE KITCHEN**! Does that word make you cringe and want to run?

Join me in learning some very practical tips to have an enjoyable time in the kitchen.

Is your kitchen the daily hub of activity, where everyone is rushing through grabbing food and running out the door, stuffing their face as they go? Or is it a relaxed atmosphere that's warm and welcoming, where friends can sit and chat over a cup of coffee and feel right at home?

One of my biggest pet peeves is a messy kitchen with cluttered counters. In fact, when I go to the kitchen to prepare food, I will clear a counter and wipe it down just so I can start out with a clean work area and have a lot of elbow room

Here's a list of some things you can do daily to keep your kitchen cheery and homey:
- **Light a candle...**

...I learned that lighting a candle gives your kitchen a cozy, welcoming feeling! It has a way of softening the mood and making that when your friends drop by they will feel welcome to 'sit a spell'. Whenever you walk past your candle during the day and notice it, take a moment to say a prayer of peace over your loved ones and your home!

- **Turn on soft music...**

...Turning on soft music makes a world of a difference in this home. When the day is getting long and the kids are wearing on your nerves, turn on some soft worship music and bask in the presence of God. It has a way of calming down this rushed feeling we tend to have and helps us remember that God has it all under control.

- **Wash the dirty dishes... (or put them in the dishwasher)**

...Washing the dirty dishes (or putting them in the dishwasher) is a feeling of accomplishment in itself! It's refreshing to walk into the kitchen and that huge stack of dirty dishes that was there, is just gone. I like to fill my dishwasher during the day, and then in the evening I will finish loading it and run it while we are in bed. Then it is ready to be emptied in the morning when we get up.

- **Wipe the counters and oven...**

...A dirty oven seems to be most women's worst nightmare. I think these glass tops are especially harder to keep clean. I would encourage you to wipe your counters and oven on a daily basis just to help with germs and keep away fruit flies...

- **Sweep up the crumbs...**

...Keeping the floor clean is a key thing for me. My husband hates having dirty floors and so do I. Since our kitchen is always cold I wear socks a lot and it's my pet-peeve to step in some sticky crumbs that want to stick to the bottom of my feet every time I take a step.

- **Bake something that lights up the whole house with delicious aromas...**

...the smell of fresh baked bread, bars, cookies, cakes, or

anything for that matter, have a way of making your whole house smell delicious and inviting! Most husbands will enjoy coming home to sweet smells wafting through the house.

- **Clean up after yourself...**

...I find it a lot easier to clean up the dishes and put away the ingredients that I used while preparing food as soon as I'm done with it, rather than an hour later coming back and having to clean it up. It's too much like starting over for me then....

- **Include your kids...**

...Yes it takes longer and makes more messes but having your kids occasionally help you in the kitchen. It gives you a chance to teach them the art of cooking/baking and is also an opportunity to teach them to work with someone else. My daughter already loves sticking her nose into everything I do if she has a half chance.

Do you struggle with finding your way around in the kitchen? Meal planning? Cooking?

Here are several ideas of ways to find someone to mentor you and help you get started, I really enjoy cooking and baking and would love for you to start enjoying it today too!

o First, pray about it and ask God to show you who He put out there to be your mentor, trust me He cares about little details like that and already knows who He wants you to contact.

o Find a friend that is good at cooking and ask her if she would be interested in mentoring you.

o Is there a family member that seems to be talented in that area that you would feel comfortable with? See if they would be interested in helping you get started, or giving you meal ideas and recipes

o Is there an older lady at church that has extra time and would be glad to have something to do? Ask her.

o (This is a little stretch for me, *smiles*) but email me at leah@w2wministries.org, I would be happy to help you get started and give you ideas and tips. I am by no means a 'seasoned' cook but I enjoy cooking and baking and am blessed to have grown up learning a lot of the basics at a young age so I could at least try to help you get started.

One important thing about finding a mentor to help you...

Be sure to find someone that you feel completely comfortable with. It should be someone that you are free to email, call, text, or chat with at any time and ask them simple questions, knowing they enjoy helping you, and that they love watching you grow and learn all these skills!

Everyone has different ideas and you will need to find out what you are capable of doing for your family, but be willing to learn from whomever you chose as your mentor. It is hard to mentor someone that isn't willing to learn and take advice.

Most of all, RELAX and HAVE FUN, with your mentor, and in the kitchen.

Do you already enjoy cooking and baking and want to reach out and bless someone else that is struggling in this area?

Then they can urge the younger women to love their husbands and children, to be self-controlled and pure, to be busy at home, to be kind, and to be subject to their husbands, so that no one will malign the word of God. Titus 2:4-5

Here are several ideas of teaching new wives and

mothers the joys of cooking...

- Get to know them personally, what do they enjoy? Likes, dislikes, etc...
- Find out what they already know and what they want to learn
- Have a party for a few of your friends and cook or bake something, giving them tips as you work.
- Share your simple and delicious recipes with them so they can start out with easy recipes, and won't get discouraged as quickly.
- Have a party and let them cook and you will be there to answer questions they may have as they are doing it.
- Offer to babysit her kids so she can cook a nice meal for her husband
- Fill a basket with the basic essentials needed in the kitchen and give it to a friend that is wanting to start baking more but feeling overwhelmed. **
- Have you ever heard of Cookie mix in a jar? (Click the link to check it out.) Make a bunch of these and pass them out to busy mothers. Hint: they make great gifts for party hostess' or even Birthdays, Thinking of you's, Christmas, etc etc...
- Get a list of her family's favorite dishes, find the recipes, cook the meal and invite her family over for the evening, enjoy each other's company, eat, and then share the recipes with her and give her tips on how you made everything.

**Here are some ideas of things that are used quite frequently in this house:

Flour – sugar – oil – brown sugar – baking soda – baking

powder – vanilla extract – oatmeal – salt – pepper – seasoning salt (that's my favorite ingredient LOL) – ketchup – mustard – onions – potatoes – carrots – cream cheese – sour cream – milk

Anyways, you get the idea... click here to see a full list of many more items that are essential.

Are you a mother of teenage daughter(s)? Do you have nieces? Granddaughters? That you want to help learn their way around in the kitchen?

Try some of these ideas:

❖ Start out with something as simple as making a cake (cake mix is even easier) It will boost her confidence and make her want to try other things.

❖ Praise her for wanting to learn and show recognition for her efforts, even if it flops, be encouraging, help her figure out what she did wrong and remind her, there is always tomorrow to start over. (I made enough 'flops' in my day, just a simple thing like forgetting the baking soda or baking powder in a cake)

❖ Let her find a completely new recipe to both of you and work together to make it, this can also be a time of bonding and finding out what is going on in her life.

❖ Let her plan a full course meal and prepare everything that is needed, be there to answer questions, but let her make the meal, and don't be surprised if dinner is late, it will take her longer then you.

❖ Share some stories of your failures and successes, there's nothing better than knowing that the great cook Mama is now, also had some flops and lessons to learn along the way.

❖ Let her cook a surprise meal for the whole family, no

one knows what's for dinner until you get to the table,

❖ Praise her for a job well done, even if the food isn't like yours, with a few tries, and knowing you believe in her, she'll be competing with you for the best meal in no time at all.

❖ Finally, let her plan a party and decorate and invite her friends over for the evening. Brag to her friends on how well she is doing in the kitchen; enjoy a fun evening of getting to know her friends and playing games. (You may even want to send the guys to town for their dinner and have a girls evening.)

❖ Invite their friends over for a cooking party, let them each bring a recipe with the ingredients that they want to make and be there giving encouragement and direction as needed.

My biggest thrust in this all is **PRAISE**, (in case you haven't picked that up yet) most kids thrive in knowing they are doing a good job, and it will boost their confidence so much in knowing that someone (they value your opinion even if they act like they don't) believes in them and has confidence that they can do this!

Here is a simple recipe for Double Chocolate Banana Muffins that I thought you might like to try. They are delicious and it's hard to stop at just one. At least they don't last long around here.

Double Chocolate Banana Muffins

3 c. flour
2 c. sugar
½ c. cocoa powder
2 tsp soda
1 tsp salt
½ tsp baking powder
2 2/3 c. mashed bananas
2/3 c. vegetable oil
2 eggs
2 c. chocolate chips

leahscooking.com · Woman to Woman Ministries

Preheat oven to 350*.

Mix flour, sugar, cocoa powder, soda, salt and baking powder together.

Add the mashed bananas, oil and eggs and beat well with a hand beater. (you can mix by hand as well just make sure its mixed really well).

Fold in the chocolate chips.

Put cupcake liners into your muffin tins and fill them about half full of batter.

Hint: Using a large cookie scoop to fill the cupcake liners is so much easier than a spoon and a lot less mess.

This recipe makes approximately 2 dozen cupcakes.

Bake for 15 -20 minutes or until toothpick inserted the middle comes out clean.

Enjoy!!

Living Titus 2
Faith With One Another
By Alyssa Santos

The air slammed my face and stung my eyes as I grabbed the dogs' leashes and opened the front door. Gusts of wind like knife-blades cut through the ice-cold morning air slapping my cheeks and finding ways into my clothing, down my collar. I wanted to turn back inside and curl up by the fire with an old movie or a well-loved book. Even doing an aerobic video in my living room seemed more inviting than hoofing it through my neighborhood turned tundra. But, I was committed to walking and taking the corgis out for their exercise and they pulled at the leashes, ready to go. Their fur coats and low-to-the-ground profile preserved them from the worst of the wind.

I chose my route with the big hill because it's also the shortest. The sun flooded my path and the blue skies rolled endless above me, but there was no warmth, no birdsong, just the whoosh of winter wind and an occasional skittering of a brittle maple leaf scraping across the pavement. The warmth of my breath trapped in my scarf and fogged my sunglasses and my muscles, stiff with cold, moved reluctantly at my demand. The sun burned in its usual place but failed to give heat, failed to penetrate the air chilled and whipped icy in the arctic. No cosmic accident or failure caused this phenomenon of contrasts; there were no sun flares, nor had we migrated away from our celestial center, it's just a fact that in some places on Earth the sun can gaze its brilliant eye upon us and we're still freezing. It's called winter. And it makes me pick up my pace and hit a quick stride and get back home.

I didn't suffer frostbite. In fact, my morning walk generated a lot of heat in my body (good calorie burning) and as for my fingers and cheeks and nose, well, they weren't beyond the warming reach a steaming cup of tea and a furnace. Nicely thawed, I thought of my life-walk with God and how different, yet similar, it is to my daily walks. I may not have wounds and scars from my morning walks, and in fact, when I am committed to facing the elements daily, I am better off physically. But walking day after day, with God, can be a little like my winter walk that morning. God's light—his brilliance—never fades. He always remains my soul-center just as the Sun is our solar system's center. But sometimes, the clouds move in and shield its light from me. Sometimes the barren seasons, like winter, seem lifeless and cold and uninviting. But, in spite of the atmosphere surrounding me, I am always better off walking with God.

Oftentimes, Christians refer to choosing to follow God and the teachings of the Bible as their "walk with God." The apostle Paul sometimes referred to it as a race. Always, our movement should be forward. Jeremiah, the prophet of the Old Testament, who ministered to Judah, leveled with God's people about their disobedience and repeated choices to ignore God's promises and his commands. He gives great insight into the importance of one's faith walk and which direction a person might go if she chooses her own way:

"For in the day that I brought them out of the land of Egypt, I did not speak to your fathers or command them concerning burnt offerings and sacrifices. But this command I gave them: 'Obey my voice, and I will be your God, and you shall be my people. And walk in all the way that I command you, that it may be well with you.' But they did not obey or incline their ear, but walked in their own counsels and the stubbornness of their evil hearts, and went backward and not forward." Jeremiah 7:22-14 ESV

According to Bible history, God rescued the Hebrew people from Egypt and the tyranny of slavery they endured under the Egyptian rule (see: Exodus). He gathered at least one million men into a nation free and offered to be their God, to lead them and be present with them day and night. The unique glory of God, called Shekinah Glory, dwelled in the pillar of fire and a cloud that led them out of Egypt (Exodus 13:21-22). He invited them to be his people and offered to be their God. He offered them freedom and a new life in a prosperous and verdant land. He offered them protection and provision. He wanted to meet all of their needs. In exchange, He asked that they recognize their need (as individuals and corporately) for Him and listen to his voice, choose to obey his voice and walk in the way that He instructed them. Jeremiah notes here that had they in fact cooperated with the powerful God that rescued them that it would "be well" with them.

But they did not obey nor listen. They walked according to their own morality and desires; the persistent stubbornness of evil in their hearts led them backward instead of forward. Our walk, like the Hebrew people of the Bible, must compel us forward. If, in fact, we are heading backward, it's safe to say that we are not actually walking with God, but according to our own ideas.

In Paul's letter to Titus, a trusted leader who was heading to the island of Crete to instruct the believers there, he addresses what the New Testament forward movement should look like. On first glance, this compact letter might look like a dry list of to-do's and not-to-do's all about how to be a good Christian community. But taken at that surface level, all that might be accomplished by the Cretans is that they might establish a very moral group of people intentionally doing life together. But morality, or good life choices according to one's own set of standards, is so much less than Paul, or God, intended for the Cretan church—and for us. Consider the first lines of the letter:

"Paul, a servant of God and an apostle of Jesus Christ for the faith of God's elect and the knowledge of the truth that leads to godliness—a faith and a knowledge resting on the hope of eternal life, which God, who does not lie, promised before the beginning of time, and at his appointed season he brought his word to light through the preaching entrusted to me by the command of God our Savior." Titus 1:1-3 NIV

Paul's basis of instruction came from God, but it was delivered with the ultimate goal that the individuals in the church of Crete become mature: beginning with faith, then knowledge, then godliness. In the end, the people would be marked by hope of eternal life, promised by God and secured by Jesus Christ, and onto this hope they could pin their faith and knowledge. Godliness is the produce, the inevitable outcome of a life energized and moving forward by faith in God and knowledge of Him and His character.

Enoch, an Old Testament character who was briefly mentioned in Genesis and then given a place in the New Testament "Faith Hall of Fame" in Hebrews, was said to have walked with God (Genesis 5) and to have pleased him (Hebrews 11). Enoch walked right into the presence of God. We know few details, but it could be concluded that Enoch listened to and obeyed God, as well. Godliness, then, involves faith in God through Jesus Christ, knowledge of the character of God, listening to his voice through the Word we call the Bible, and leaving our own counsel (ideas) aside and obeying

God, and walking (forward, daily, consistently).

So then, to keep the instructions that were laid out in the book of Titus from becoming burdensome and laborious (and legalistic!), God has provided us with helpers to keep up our energy and refine our focus on the goal, which is maturity as believers in Jesus Christ living out godly lives defined by our faith, knowledge and hope.

Our first helper is God Himself! The Holy Spirit was the promised person of God that would come and dwell within (not just alongside of or ahead of us) everyone who professed faith in Jesus Christ.

"If you love me, you will keep my commandments. And I will ask the Father, and he will give you another Helper, to be with you forever, even the Spirit of truth, whom the world cannot receive, because it neither sees him nor knows him. You know him, for he dwells with you and will be in you. But the Helper, the Holy Spirit, whom the Father will send in my name, he will teach you all things and bring to your remembrance all that I have said to you." John 14:15-17, 26 ESV

Our second helper is community: the family of believers that began with the disciples, those who first walked with God in accordance with Jesus Christ and began the loving God, loving Jesus movement we call the church.

"A new command I give you: Love one another. As I have loved you, so you must love one another. By this all men will know that you are my disciples, if you love one another." John 13:34-35 NIV

"But you are the ones chosen by God, chosen for the high calling of priestly work, chosen to be a holy people, God's instruments to do his work and speak out for him, to tell others of the night-and-day difference he made for you—from nothing to something, from rejected to accepted." 1 Peter 2:9-10 MSG

"Each of you should use whatever gift you have received to serve others, as faithful stewards of God's grace in its various forms. If anyone speaks, they should do so as one who speaks the very words of God. If anyone serves, they should do so with the strength God

provides, so that in all things God may be praised through Jesus Christ. To him be the glory and the power forever and ever. Amen."
1 Peter 4:10-11 NIV

"Likewise, teach the older women to be reverent in the way they live, not to be slanderers or addicted to much wine, but to teach what is good. Then they can train the younger women to love their husbands and children, to be self-controlled and pure, to be busy at home, to be kind, and to be subject to their husbands, so that no one will malign the word of God." Titus 2:3-5 NIV

"Therefore, since we are surrounded by so great a cloud of witnesses, let us also lay aside every weight, and sin which clings so closely, and let us run with endurance the race that is set before us."
Hebrews 12:1 NIV

It is apparent from these selections of the New Testament that community is an important ingredient in our forward-moving walk with God. In this community we are to find love, cooperation, active and effective service to God through serving others, good teaching, mentorship, modeling, wisdom, goodness, purpose and joy in the roles we each have in our homes, communities, churches and in the world. We are, in a sense, to do this walking together. It's not a solo activity.

Perhaps you've been hurt or disappointed, rejected or confused by the community in your life. Perhaps you're new to this walking with God thing and it all sounds like too much effort, too much groovy-hippie-like commune stuff or you simply don't know where to begin. Just like taking a big, long walk, it comes first by making the decision to go for a walk, putting on those walking shoes and taking the first steps. I want to encourage you to take your focus off of the circumstances or the past hurts or mistakes and fix your eyes on Jesus, who loves you, who authored your faith since the beginning of time and take those first steps.

When Jesus is our focus, when we are listening to the sound of the voice we know to be His through His Word and Spirit, we find our feet know where to go. A few years ago, my family went to visit relatives who live in Pebble Beach, the beautiful seaside community nestled beneath the cypress and eucalyptus trees alongside the Pacific Ocean. We arrived at nighttime and I awoke early in the morning, before anyone else. I slipped on my sneakers and pulled on a sweatshirt and snuck out of the front door. Anxious for a glimpse of the breathtaking blue of the Monterey Coast, I put feet to pavement and followed the sound of the waves. I knew I was about two miles away but felt confident I could make the right turns by following the rhythmic roar of the rolling surf. I was rewarded by a dazzling sight of the rising sun dancing off of the waves, the scent of salt and fresh oceanic wind in my face. I arrived at the seaside with tears in my eyes, happy to be dazzled, happy to have made the early walk.

The long walk through this lifetime can take us on many unexpected turns and unplanned detours and we get tripped up on more distractions than we can count, so the community of helpers is both vital and priceless in the quality and movement of our walk with God. I remember a time when I was feeling very alone and discouraged. I was mourning the loss of several friendships that had broken apart and a well-loved relationship with my own sister that had reached an impasse so great I doubted it could ever be breached, even with God's grace. God met me in this season of solitude, however, and looking back I cherish that time I had alone with Him healing my fissured places. One day, after months of seeking Him alone, my husband and I sat behind a couple at church that looked to be about twenty years older than us. We visited for a bit after church and she mentioned that she led a journaling-based life group on Tuesdays. I mentioned that I liked to write, but never had the time because I had a lot going on raising four kids. She invited me anyway. I was tentative, afraid even, since I had recently experienced so much heartache. But my husband urged me on and even said, "If you don't like it, if you think they're weird, you don't have to go again!"

On a cold, winter evening, I walked into the church nursery, the room available for us to meet, and there we rocked in time with the words and the Word and I found comfort, community, a group of caring women (most older than I) who loved the gift of writing and accepted one another. They drew me in with grace and held me carefully in arms of community that I had not known before. I found my ecclesia, my family. Over the next several years they have become important as a group and as individuals because they took the instructions in Titus 2 joyfully into their hearts and lives and loved me to health simply by teaching me how to walk in faith again. I have found purpose and joy in my life; I have found a voice and meaning in writing again; I have found a confidence that I can share with others—all because of a small group of walking, listening, obeying women.

In 2011, I nearly died in a car collision. My left leg was shattered and after months of not bearing any weight, my doctor determined the time had come in my healing process to begin to place weight upon it, little by little. At first, the pain was unbearable, because bone pain is deep. My muscles were weak from months of disuse. In time, as physical therapy and many, many exercises strengthened my body; I was finally able to try to walk again. I leaned heavily into my therapist's arm and took a wobbly step. Eventually, I could take steps alone. But, I had a long way to go because in the time that had passed, my muscles had forgotten how to do the walking process correctly. I needed support, needed correction and assistance and opportunities to grow stronger so that I would, one day, walk strong and without a limp.

I felt like a baby, watching my physical therapist walk correctly in order to show me how to follow her body motions. I felt silly, like I should know better, do better, walk better. But I learned as I was relearning to walk that the process of becoming a walker can be slow. I learned to grace myself with permission to rest when I was tired, to cry when I needed to, to laugh at myself. The process of learning to walk again taught me this: in walking with God, I need to have a mentor, someone whom I can learn from and follow. There are times when I have a hard time listening and need to be reminded. There are times I really want my own way and need to be corrected. There are times I want to be proud of my stride and my accomplishments and I need to be submissive to the greater goal, which is a god-pleasing life like Enoch's that will be inviting to others.

Learning to walk again created a compassion in me for others who might be, for various reasons, struggling, lonely, hurt or afraid. I need to slow down and join hands and hearts with others that God leads into my life. I need to pray for opportunities to teach what I've learned about listening to, obeying, following and walking with God. And finally, I learned that He allowed my leg to heal and strengthen and allowed me to grow strong enough to walk limp-free, so that I might be the outstretched arm and voice of encouragement to someone who desperately needs my empathy and help as they pursue walking with God.

The Titus 2 concepts of mentorship are best expressed in an authentic walk with God. When we choose to be honest with one another and vulnerable, when our goal is to hold fast that faith in Jesus and pursue knowledge of Him together, when our hope is pinned on Him and we listen, obey and follow after him together, we can't help but be joyful and real. Then our lives will become like the call of the ocean, the invitation to community and the strong, supportive arm others need so that they, too, might know Jesus and find a "faith and knowledge resting on the hope of eternal life which God...promised before the beginning of time".

Living Titus 2 in Your Walk with God
By Jenifer Metzger

Have you ever opened the Bible and simply felt overwhelmed? Not quite sure where to start and struggle to understand? There is so much to know and do, where do you start? God didn't save us only to walk away and leave us alone. He gives us two incredible helpers: the Holy Spirit and mature Christians. Mature Christians are incredible people who have been saved longer than we have and can become a mentor to help us grow in our walk with God. But how do we find these mature Christians who are willing to guide us along?

The first step is to pray. Ask God to send someone into your life who can be your mentor in your walk with God. Ask God for someone to come along side you and encourage you. God wants this for you, therefore when you ask, He will honor that prayer. Then look around your church or your Bible study group. Is there a woman living her life for Jesus, someone seeking after the heart of the Father? This doesn't have to be a woman older than you. It simply needs to be someone who is farther along in her walk with God, someone who is where you want to be in your spiritual growth. Go to her. Tell her what your desire and ask her if she would be willing to walk along side you and be your mentor.

The beauty of having a mentor in your walk with God is having a sister and friend all rolled in to one beautiful package and creating a life-long connection with her. As she invests into your life, your friendship with grow and deepen and become a relationship that you cherish.

However, it may not always be easy. By having a mentor, you are inviting a sister in Christ into your life. You are asking her to show you the truth in love. You are giving her permission to call you out when you need to be called out. And you are allowing her to be real with you. If she sees something in your life and comes to you in love, don't be upset with her. Remember that this is what you wanted, what you needed; someone to walk with you and help you. Let her speak to you and simply listen to what is on her heart. Make it a point to learn and move forward. The moment we become offended, we emotionally shut down and the mentorship is negatively affected. Having someone mentor us means being willing to have our feelings hurt for a few moments when it means growth is around the corner.

No matter how long you have been saved, three months or thirty years, we all need someone to look up to. This side of Heaven, we will never 'arrive.' There is always something new to learn and always room for growth.

Meeting with your mentor.

Make regular meetings with your mentor. This could be coffee dates, phone calls, or emails. The point is to meet regularly so that she gets a good glimpse into your life and knows how to help you along. Be open and honest with her. When you question something in the Bible, talk to her about it. When you are struggling with something God is talking to you about, share with her. If you are quiet and never bring forth your questions, concerns and struggles, she will be unable to help you grow.

Consider sending her a text or email each day after you have spent time with God in prayer and Bible reading. This is an excellent way to be held accountable. In the busyness of life we sometimes struggle to find time with God. But knowing that someone is waiting to hear that you had that quiet time is a help. I have been immensely blessed with my Morning Reflections group. Morning Reflections is my accountability group and each morning after we have our quiet time, we share where we read in the Bible and something God is showing us. It is wonderful to know those women are there waiting to hear from me.

What if my mentor messes up?

Remember that we are not perfect. We are human. Your mentor will mess up from time to time. We are all a work in progress while on this earth. So don't write off the relationship and mentorship just because she slipped up. Pray for her. Offer her grace. After all, God offers you grace.

Me? A mentor?

Yes, you. A mentor. We are called by God to come along side the younger women and train them. This may not necessarily mean younger in years. In some cases it may just mean you have been a Christian longer than someone. The world's view of what a woman should be is very different than God's view. The world tells us to stand on our own two feet. Be strong and independent. God wants us to rely on Him. The world says outward beauty is of high importance. God says look at the heart. The world tells women different than what God wants. We need to come along side women, especially the newer believers, and guide them. Encourage them. Show them God's way. And you, friend, can do that.

I know, I know. You don't think you can. I understand. The idea of someone looking up to me can be a bit overwhelming at times. I never want to lead anyone astray, appear that I 'know it all' or hurt someone's feelings. So how can I possibly be a Titus 2 woman? By letting God lead me.

Becoming a mentor.

There are many ways to become a Titus 2 mentor to young women. Is there a new believer in your church? She will need someone to come alongside her as a mentor. Is there a new woman in your Bible study group who hasn't been saved as long as you? Chances are she needs someone to mentor her. Maybe a woman has just moved into your neighborhood, just joined your child's play group, or is a fellow baseball mom with you. Good chance she could be looking for someone to look up to.

Where do I start?

Prayer. Prayer is always the key. Ask God to make you into the woman He wants you to be so that you can mentor other women as they grow to what God wants them. Then pray and ask God to lead you to the lady He wants you mentor. Let God lead you each step of the way.

Mentorship doesn't mean perfection. Simply because you step into the role of a mentor does not mean you suddenly must be the perfect woman. She, this perfect woman, does not exist. What it does mean is that you strive to live a life pleasing and honoring to God and as you do this, you encourage others to do the same.

Once you have prayed and God has led you to the woman, or sometimes women, that He wants you to mentor, talk to her. Maybe she is seeking mentorship and you can move forward. Or maybe the idea is new to her and she isn't sure what to expect. Invite her over to your home for coffee and dessert, or maybe out to lunch. Discuss the idea of mentorship with her. Give her your ideas and share your heart openly with her. Then pray together and give her time to respond.

Once your mentee is ready to begin a mentorship, decide how often and how you will meet. Will you meet weekly for coffee? Or perhaps weekly over the phone and monthly for lunch? Decide what works best for both of you, then stick to it.

Pray daily for her. Pray that God would move her into a new understanding of Him and that He would draw her into a deep relationship with Him.

Be available to her day and night. Now when it comes to being available, I want to be upfront about something. You need to be available to her at all times. It is important in a mentorship that your mentee knows you are there for them. But you also need to be there for your own family. You may want to establish some guidelines. Such as, if it is something that can wait until morning, do not call in the middle of the night. But if it is a spiritual emergency, the middle of the night call is okay. Or tell her to leave you a message if you do not answer the phone and you will get back to her as soon as you can. Or if you work and cannot take calls at work, maybe you need her to shoot you a text that simply says *call when you can*. Be available, but be sure you are both of the same understanding as to what that means.

Have Bible studies together. There is something so wonderful about doing a Bible study with a sister in Christ! You both learn and grow together. But when you are mentoring someone, you are able to teach her as you go along. You can do devotional studies or simply dig right into the Word. One great way to learn the Bible is to use the S.O.A.P. Method. That is Scripture, read the verses and write them out. Observe, write down one or two observations from the reading. Application, write down how you can apply it to your life now. And pray about it. This is a great method for learning the Word and works very well as you are leading someone.

Ask her questions. Lots of questions. Make her think. This method is called coaching and is something my husband absolutely loves! Ask her questions about why she thinks that way or why she does something. It really gets you to do some soul searching and thinking and is a great way to learn.

Help her set goals. Maybe she has never read the Bible. Encourage her to read one chapter a day for one month. Check in on her regularly to see how she is doing with her goal. Once she has hit the goal, encourage her do more. Or set a goal of only listening to Christian music for one month. Check in and see how she is doing. Help her find Christian music she likes so that she is able to stick to the goal. We all grow when we set reachable goals. So help her out!

How to handle the sticky situations.

Here's the hard part of mentorship, calling them out. In this particular chapter we are talking about mentorship in our walk with God. Has your mentee been missing church, using bad language, or gossiping? These, and other situations, are reasons for you to step in. But listen to me very closely here. You must do it in *love*. If you do not handle this with care, you can damage the relationship you have built.

Before going to her, make sure you have the facts straight. Personally, I can never judge whether someone is in a Sunday church service or not. I am a children's pastor and most weeks I am in the children's room when people arrive at church and still there when they leave. I never know who is at church and who is not. So before saying to someone that they have been missing, I need to ask them. So get the facts straight before you say anything. Next pray. Ask God to help you handle this with grace and love. Then go to her in private, not around others. Tell her your concerns. Ask her how you can help her, and truly be there for her. And lastly, never tell others. Part of mentoring someone is that everything she says to you stays with you.

As a mentor, you will come across these situations. Handle them with care and you will both grow.

Having a mentor in your spiritual walk with benefit you in beautiful ways. You will learn and grow from someone who has already been following God for some time. You be encouraged from their knowledge of the Lord. In the same aspect, being a mentor to someone will bless you as you teach someone else. It's time to be Titus 2 women and come alongside one another.

About the Authors

Jenifer Metzger, W2W founder and co-leader ~ Jenifer and her husband, Jeremy, have been married for sixteen years and have four children whom she calls her blessings from Heaven. She is a house wife and homeschooling mom. Jenifer's husband is the children's pastor at their church and she enjoys serving alongside him. Jenifer is a woman learning to say yes to God and excited with the journey He is taking her on. Jenifer blogs at www.jenifermetzger.org and you can email her at jenifer@w2wministries.org.

Debi Baker, W2W co-leader ~ Debi and her husband, Jim, have been married for thirty-seven years. She is a wife, mother, grandmother, office manager, and Pastor. Debi desires to be used by God. Having been a Christian for over thirty years, she says she is just now learning that she is special to God. Knowing and believing are two different things. She says she's always known...but she is just starting to believe it. Debi is learning to say "Yes!" to God. She is addicted to her family and loves spending time with them. Debi and Jim enjoy traveling on their Goldwing motorcycle...it's an amazing way to see this glorious creation of ours. You can find Debi at www.debibaker.org and you can email her at debi@w2wministries.org.

Jenilee Goodwin ~ Jenilee and her husband, Jeremy, are missionaries to Sengeal, West Africa. They have been married for twelve years and have three amazing daughters joining them on their adventurous traveling life! Jeniliee loves the outlet that social media gives her to connect with other women about topics close to her heart. Parenting, family, motherhood and marriage are all right at the top of the topics list! God has given each of us an incredible journey and Jenilee enjoys that journey with women in real, practical, fun ways. You can find Jenilee blogging at www.ourgoodwinjourney.com and email her at jenilee@w2wministries.org

Leah Hostetler, W2W co-leader ~ Leah and her husband Owen have been married for 2 ½ years and have one daughter who is their pride and joy. She is a house wife and also makes and sells cookies for Amish Sweets whenever she has time. She is learning the joys and blessings God gives her when she say 'Yes' to Him and is excited to embrace the calling He has

on her life. You can find her blogging, bragging on her girl, and sharing recipes at Leah's Cooking at www.leahscooking.com. You can email Leah at leah@w2wministries.org.

Shari Miller, Shari is wife to her husband, Bill, and mother to two precious gifts from God. She is a stage IV breast cancer survivor and lives each day striving to give God the glory for all that He has done in her life. You can find Shari blogging about leaving a Godly legacy, hope and encouragement in Jesus and her life's journey at Leaving A Legacy. You can find Leaving a Legacy at www.shariamiller.com and email Shari at shariannmiller@gmail.com.

Lisa Shaw ~ Lisa knows that Jesus' love is the story of her life. She's a Speaker, Christian Consultant, Author, Radio Host and an ordained Pastor, who uses the gifts God has given to her to help build the lives of women for sixteen years. Lisa knows what it is to be a wounded woman but she also knows what it means to experience His restorative power  upon her life. She has a heart for seeing women live in the wholeness God has provided for them through Christ. Lisa believes the quote: "People don't care how much you know until they know how much you care." She cares. Lisa is grateful to be married to her husband Peter Shaw. They have two adult children, two grandchildren and one son-in-law all of whom she loves very much. They reside in Florida. You can find Lisa blogging at www.lisashawcares.com.

Alyssa Santos ~ Finding faith, purpose and freedom as a writer, encourager, wife, mom, gardener and somewhat reformed pew-rat. Alyssa always thought of herself as an ordinary girl. She says she is still just the girl-next-door, but has come to realize that we are, none of us, ordinary. She has embraced that she is God's handiwork and an important part of His plan to love and redeem this world. Alyssa's aim in her life and writing is to share grace and abundant joy through a personal and meaningful relationship with Jesus Christ. You can find Alyssa blogging at www.alyssasantos.com.

Jami Balmet ~ Jami is passionate about Biblical Homemaking and striving to be a woman of God. Jami and her loving husband, Jason, recently welcomed twin baby boys into their home. She has a heart for hospitality and making her home an inviting place that reflects Christ. She blogs about this passion at Young Wife's Guide. She

is also passionate about creating a healthy and thriving home and shares recipes, tips and tutorials at Homemaking from Scratch. You can find her at www.youngwifesguide.com and www.homemakingfromscratch.com.

For more encouragement on how to live a Titus 2 life and much more, visit Woman to Woman Ministries at www.w2wministries.org or check us out on Facebook.

Made in the USA
Lexington, KY
21 August 2014